Declut
And
Organize

Live Intentionally by Decluttering Your Home and Life, Doing More With Less and Focusing on What is Essential in Your Life

By Matt Mckinney

© **Copyright 2019 - All rights reserved.**

The content contained within this book may not be reproduced, duplicated or transmitted without direct written permission from the author or the publisher.

Under no circumstances will any blame or legal responsibility be held against the publisher or author for any damages, reparation, or monetary loss due to the information contained within this book. Either directly or indirectly.

Legal Notice:

This book is copyright protected. This book is only for personal use. You cannot amend, distribute, sell, use, quote or paraphrase any part, or the content within this book, without the consent of the author or publisher.

Disclaimer Notice:

Please note the information contained within this document is for educational and entertainment purposes only. All effort has been executed to present accurate, up to date and reliable, complete information. No warranties of any kind are declared or implied. Readers acknowledge that the author is not engaging in the rendering of legal, financial, medical or professional advice. The content within this book has been derived from various sources. Please consult a licensed professional before attempting any techniques outlined in this book.

By reading this document, the reader agrees that under no circumstances is the author responsible for any losses, direct or indirect, which are incurred as a result of the use of information contained within this document, including, but not limited to, —errors, omissions, or inaccuracies.

Table of Contents

Introduction 1

Chapter 1: The Pitfalls of Clutter 3

    What is involved? 5

Chapter 2: You Can Take Action Against The Clutter 8

    Why is Doing This Necessary? 9

Chapter 3: Understand What's Going On 12

    Sign of a Cluttered Life: Angst 13

    Sign of a Cluttered Life: Anxiety 14

    Sign of a Cluttered Life: It's Never Enough 14

    Sign of a Cluttered Life: You are Never Satisfied 16

    Sign of a Cluttered Life: You are Scared You Will Lose Everything 16

    Start by Figuring out What Matters to You 17

    Value Audit 18

    Do a Detox 19

Chapter 4: How to Start 21

    Change You Personal Patterns 23

    Just Do It! 25

    Don't Forget What is Important 26

Don't Skip Anything 27

Chapter 5: Getting Rid of Mental Clutter 29

The Bottom Line 34

Harmful Emotional Habit # 1: Regularly comparing yourself to other people 36

Harmful Emotional Habit # 2: Drawing Mental Prizes from Material Belongings 38

Harmful Emotional Habit # 3: Immediately Thinking that a Hefty Price Tag Indicates Higher Value 41

Harmful Emotional Habit # 4: Focusing on "Drawing Out" the Benefits People Have Rather Than Viewing Them as Whole People 47

Hazardous Emotional Habit # 5: Freeloading Emotionally Off People 50

Harmful Personality Type # 1: The Black Hole 52

Harmful Personality Type # 2: The Judge 53

Harmful Personality Type # 3: The Stylish Hoarder 54

Toxic Personality Type # 4: The Troll 57

Chapter 6: Getting Rid of Emotional Clutter 61

Look for and Destroy Anti Affirmations 68

How to Create Affirmations That Actually Work as They Should 77

Chapter 7: How to Get Rid of Clutter in Your Career 79

Decide to Love What You Do 80

Discovering the Courage to Let Go 87

Unlocking the Power of Passive Online Income 90

Chapter 8: How to Enjoy More with Less 94

Strip Down the Things You Enjoy 96

Uncovering the Core of Enjoyment 97

Whatever You Do ... Do This 100

Unlocking the Power of Memories 101

Chapter 9: Learn to Be Content 105

Enough is Possible 106

Achieving Emotional Contentment 107

Psychological Contentment 109

Spiritual Contentment 110

Letting Go of Attachments 111

Overcome These Enemies of Personal Change 113

Conclusion 117

Thank you for purchasing this book and I hope that you will find it beneficial. If you will want to share your thoughts on this book, you can do so by leaving a review on the Amazon page, it helps me out a lot.

Introduction

Most people buy things which they don't need to impress people they don't like at all. That's the life of most people. It may sound harsh, but it's true. People think that having more makes the life somehow better.

Quality of life is measured by what is owned. Some people also base their self worth on their possessions. You should remember that price doesn't equate value. Just because something costs more, it doesn't mean that it has more value and it will make someone's life more worthwhile.

A lot of people prioritize what is expected of them instead of what they actually want themselves. Certain values that people live by weren't even chosen by them, they were implanted by someone else.

Too many children simply live their lives based on what their parents want without any challenge or rebuttal. Maybe they don't even see that there is something to be challenged in the first place. As long as parents do and think something in a certain way, then that's all there is to it.

There isn't any inquiry into whether the whole life plan makes sense or not and whether there is a better way entirely. It is not even considered if a certain way of life makes sense in the current times. It is just assumed that a certain path is the best one since all the loved and respected people are walking it.

People in first world countries are not necessarily happy due to way too much stress and credit card debt. It seems that it's harder and harder to become content. Cluttered lives may limit the amount of joy which can be achieved in life and a lot of people aren't even aware of this.

Chapter 1: The Pitfalls of Clutter

Stress limits someone's effectiveness and it hurts relationships. The job also isn't done as well as it could be and challenges are a bigger deal than they should be. Life is not supposed to be easy and surprises are inevitable. It is all about preparation and how these surprises are handled.

However, there is a lot of entitlement and expectation that life should be smooth and easy. That is why it can be so easy to be stressed and so hard to be happy for some. The focus is always on what can be acquired in the future. Focus is placed on everything except the present, such as past failures. It is a never ending search for something to blame for why things are the way they are.

This is an example of mental clutter and a lot of people accept it as a part of life and as a statement of their self worth and their identity. In reality, mental clutter isn't something that is supposed to be a part of life and it doesn't appear by itself or by mere bad luck.

The precursor to the mental clutter is the physical clutter and this is how a never ending mental loop is established. The more mental clutter there is, the more physical clutter tends to be created. A mere sight of this causes stress and more mental clutter. This process has no end by itself.

A lot of us have no clue about this whole loop. If there is some form of unhappiness in your life, there is possibility that the source of that unhappiness could be traced back to mental clutter. This loop can prevent people for achieving happiness and other life goals.

Too many people will make excuses as they are not even aware of this loop. A resistance is also put up against any attempt to simplify things and to state how a lot of things are a little more than an unnecessary burden. The Resistance exists as a defense of the identity which is dependent on the possession of a lot of stuff.

Most people will respond to any decluttering attempt similarly. People have to want to change in order to change. Accepting that change is necessary and really internalizing that are two different things. Internalizing this fact creates urgency and that is how things really get done without justifications.

A lot of people stay stuck at simply knowing that change is necessary in order to achieve happiness and their potential in life. They also know what they should stop doing because its's wrong. It is important for this understanding to sink to the heart in order to make real progress. It is necessary to achieve true belief.

What is involved?

You are not the only one affected by clutter since you can't completely keep all the emotions to yourself which means that other people will be affected. Relationships are inevitably affected by this whole interaction between possessions and internal states. If someone is filled with harmful emotions, ideas and attitudes as a result of all the clutter, it is way too easy for something to leak out and cause things that ruin relationships such as misunderstandings and misconceptions.

Relationships won't be automatically doomed, but they may start going downhill by becoming more passive-aggressive which could cause each side to sabotage the other just for the sake of sticking it to the other side.

Relationships should be about building each other up in every way, and not about a destructive loop. Stress causes stress to spread to more people and in this way, the cycle never ends and it's like a downward spiral. This also doesn't end because people also feel that they will be in a disadvantage if they stop doing what they have always done.

Thankfully, there is a simple way to break out of this. All it takes is to be proactive and to decide to deal with clutter in order to create your ideal life. Anyone can do this regardless of their age. It is never too late or too early to start decluttering your life.

Chapter 2: You Can Take Action Against The Clutter

There is some discouragement upon the realization that a lot of issues are caused by clutter. No matter what the nature of clutter is, clutter has a lot of influence even among the most resilient people. A lot of people probably realize that they are dealing with too many things. Those things may be from the past or from the future.

There is a lot of fear and worry when it comes to decluttering. People know that too many things are bad and they don't need someone else to remind them of that. The weird thing is that people get attached to clutter to the point where they can't imagine a simpler life.

A lot of people underestimate the power of decluttering and they consider it as nothing more than an impractical speculation. The truth is that the results can be achieved by decluttering and that the positive impact can be clearly seen and accomplished by anyone.

Why is Doing This Necessary?

Even if people realize that they should declutter, they may ask themselves if it is even worth the effort although they understand that the clutter may be behind their struggle and suffering.

To the people who have already decluttred, the benefits are obvious. Decluttering enables someone to be more effective, as simple as that may sound. It's hard to be effective under constant worry and fear. Relationships also suffer because of that.

The unhappiness because of clutter manifests itself sooner or later and completely dilutes the focus. It is easier to be content by decluttering and this makes it easier to focus on what matters and this is how freedom is achieved. There is no freedom in worrying all the time about what happened or about what might happen.

You have a lot of potential and you can create the reality which you want, for better or worse. You can either box yourself in or you can create a life of freedom and possibilities for yourself.

There are steps which you can take in order to recognize all the clutter you may be dealing with. Don't skip the steps and take as much time as you need. Only move on to the next step when you have mastered the previous. Only move on to the next step when the current one becomes easy.

The steps are the following and an entire chapter is dedicated to each step. Step 1 is understanding what's going on. Step 2 is to start with what is in front of you. Step 3 is to declutter emotionally. Step 4 is to declutter psychologically. Step 5 is decluttering careerwise. Step 6 is learning how to get more out of less. Step 7 is learning how to be content.

Some flexibility can be applied to these steps since all people are different. Know what your situation is and customize accordingly. The formula which is outlined is not a perfect one and it is necessary to have self-awareness in order to make it work according to your specific circumstances.

The formula in this book is not something that will fit all sizes and you are unlikely to find anything of that sort. What is presented is more akin to the framework which requires active involvement in order to achieve personal success with decluttering.

Chapter 3: Understand What's Going On

To declutter, you have to understand what your life situation is and build a strategy around that. The strategy is focused on reducing clutter since getting rid of clutter entirely isn't possible. You will just end up disappointed if you expect to get rid of clutter entirely. Clutter reduction is the goal.

You may not have the proper perspective due to the amount of clutter around you right now and this may make it harder for you to make sense of your place in this world and your capabilities to act within it. You need a strategy for decluttering in order to stop spending money on things you don't need to impress people you don't like.

If you don't know where to start, then check your life against 5 signs of a cluttered life to see whether you are dealing with clutter. Clutter is easy to see at first, but later people get used to it and blends with the background as it becomes the default.

Decluttering should be gradual so that your perspective could adjust accordingly. You should give your perspective enough time to adjust since your attitude and relationships depend on it.

Sign of a Cluttered Life: Angst

Do you have a feeling that you are missing something no matter what you may be doing and who you may be doing it with? It feels like a piece is always missing. Something just isn't right and it is starting to mess with your head.

This feeling comes and goes. At times it is very noticeable and at times it is very subtle and you can feel it somewhere in the background. This feeling annoys you and you can't exactly put your finger on it, but you know it's there and you get used to it over time.

Sign of a Cluttered Life: Anxiety

Do you worry and think of bad scenarios too much? You worry about how people may react and how some things in the future may turn out. The reality is that things usually tend to go a lot better than the disaster you come up within your mind and you should get a sense of relief at the end. People with anxiety never feel this sense of relief and they immediately start thinking about the next disaster. It's hard to be happy or content this way.

This never ends and there is always some form of anticipation about something bad that could happen in the future. When the situation clears up, anxious people start to worry about something else. Anxiety can make people physically sick sometimes. It is necessary to have some calming ritual to get things under control.

Sign of a Cluttered Life: It's Never Enough

Have you ever thought about what makes you happy? Have you also thought about how you would be happier upon getting more of that stuff that gets you happy? A lot of people think that their life will be complete if they just got the next thing such as a new car or a bigger house or something similar.

When those things are acquired, the happiness doesn't last and inevitably people start wanting more stuff again. There is some science to this and money can make people happy, no matter what you may have been hearing. You can get a rush out of buying things, but that feeling is fleeting and after that, you will want more stuff.

This is similar to a rush from sugar or cocaine. You feel great in the beginning, but it won't last and you will try to get it again and it will never be as good as the first time. The first time you buy a car, for example, is special and it is unlikely to feel as good afterward. This all works acording to the law of diminishing returns.

It's easy to get into a routine of buying new things just to get the rush when the old things stop functioning perfectly. The first time is always like magic, though and there is a true sense of discovery and a lot of details tend to be remembered vividly for a long time.

When you buy something new, you get a rush and you are happy. It feels great, without a doubt, but it's temporary and the crash is inevitable. After the crash, the rush wants to be reexperienced and the only way is to buy more. The hole never seems to be filled and it all feels like a hamster wheel.

Sign of a Cluttered Life: You are Never Satisfied

Did you ever take the time to sit down and think about how much you have done and how much you have and concluded, based on that, that you have enough. Chances are high that the answer to that is negative. It's way easier to look over the shoulder.

What the neighbors are doing and why you aren't doing the same thing always seems to be on the mind. The grass always seems to be greener and everyone seems to be happier of Facebook.

It seems that your accomplishments, however great they may be, are never enough. There's always the feeling of more value and worth being out there. The search for bigger and shinier things never ends.

Sign of a Cluttered Life: You are Scared You Will Lose Everything

It is interesting how many people don't feel they have enough in combination with the fear of losing it all. Isn't it ironic?

These are all the signs of a cluttered life. It's hard to live a life with purpose and meaning with all the mental and physical clutter. Days just blend together without much purpose and it gets hard telling days apart and remembering much.

When life is like this from day to day, then buying stuff starts to be the only thing someone looks forward to, but after the rush had worn off, more stuff is wanted. It feels like you are running in circles with no end in sight.

Start by Figuring out What Matters to You

Now is time to figure out what is important to you. You will probably find out that stuff and possessions aren't the most important things to you. You should ask yourself what is truly important and what you would go to the end of the world for. You are the only one who can determine what is important to you based on your values and experiences.

This is a big question and some assistance may be necessary in order to get the to the answers. In order to get to those answers, you can utilize a value audit which will simplify things for you.

Value Audit

Auditing your values is simple and you don't need anything more than a piece of paper and a pen. Write down what you would do if money wasn't an issue and if you didn't care what others would think in the slightest.

Don't filter anything out and write the first thing that comes to mind. This is all about you and there are no right and wrong answers. Don't think about what others may think and try to compile a list of things that drive you. Put everything on the list without editing no matter how embarrassing or negative something may be.

What you have written down are your values and they subconsciously guide your thoughts and actions throughout the day. These values give you energy and they get you out of bed each day and give you meaning. Finding out those values is important and that is the purpose of an audit.

Do a Detox

Now that you know what is important, ask yourself why it may be important to you. It may give your life a sense of meaning or purpose. Maybe it just unleashes your imagination. It could also make you more adventurous.

You also have to ask yourself why do you like the things you like. Is it possible that your parents told you what is desirable, and how things should be done and how life is meant to be perceived? Are your perspective and your values influenced by other people?

Your values should be your choice. A lot of things you think you need may just be a result of someone else's expectations. It can be way too easy to keep doing things because that's the way they were done all along.

In order to get started, you should make a list of values that are truly yours. Next, make sure to make a list of values which you adopted externally. You detox by focusing on your own values and getting away from those which aren't yours. The decluttering starts when you let go of the external and focus on your values.

Chapter 4: How to Start

Decluterring starts with what you can see and touch. Get rid of stuff that causes any form of clutter in your life. This isn't as easy as it sounds since possessions have a way of taking hold of people. You need a plan since you may start missing things once they are gone.

You need any kind of plan since you are very likely to fail if you fail to plan. Decluttering is no exception to this. Know why you are trying to achieve what you are trying to achieve. You may come to the conclusion that your possessions are holding you back and that they are sapping your energy. It is not easy realizing that things you worked so hard for may be the main culprit.

You will realize the difficulty of decluttering when you ask yourself do you really want to get rid of a certain item even if you know that it is holding you down. It is easy to stay trapped since you may be attached to certain things emotionally.

The plan will help you realize what you are trying to accomplish and why you are doing things. Your commitment will be stronger if you write it down. When something unexpected happens, as it always does, it is way too easy to forget about priorities and that is why it is so crucial to think ahead and to write things down. Make sure to read over your writing each and every morning.

It will be inevitably hard to let some things go, but you will be good as long as you stick to your plan. Consistency is the most important thing when it comes to plans and the lack of it can be the end of even the best of plans. The sad fact is that most people fail at decluttering with carrying out their decluttering plan and it is not for the lack of resources and intelligence.

The cause of this failure is not sticking with the plan. Sticking with the plan is all it takes and there is no need to complicate it. If you have a plan, then you have clarity about what you should do each day to reach your goals. It is necessary not to deviate from the plan regardless of what may be happening.

There is bound to be a lot of resistance since most people define themselves according to their possessions. That is just how it is. When you are long enough around certain external things, those things start to define you and they can also be a limit when it comes to your capabilities. Having a plan which you can see each day is the first step

Change You Personal Patterns

It is necessary to clear up a couple of misconceptions. This book isn't about getting rid of everything and living like a monk away from the civilization. It is about changing your philosophy about stuff. Stuff has the hold of you when you start allowing it to define you as an individual.

This happens all the time and most people tend to define themselves based on consumption. Ironically, the consumption never seems to truly fulfill them. The hunger within them never ends.

You may have only been able to afford 2 simple meals a day at one point of your life. You may have been quite content with it at the time even if there were so many better things out there. That just shows that you don't necessarily need a lot of stuff to be happy as long as you have people around you who care about you and with whom you can spend quality time with. None of this requires a lot of money.

If you are not careful, your life may end up being more and more expensive and this is, in part, due to changing expectations. It's easy to think that having a luxurious apartment is the only way to get ahead and be worthy.

Every graduation and every promotion has a way of driving up the cost and it never ends. The truth is as simple as that. When you think about it, is having a Ferrari and a huge house worth all the sacrifice? That is what you have to answer yourself, but the focus should always be on what you really need. Everyone will require a personalized solution.

You can only create a plan once you start thinking about what you really need. Once you have that foundation, that is when you start creating your relationships and possessions anew.

When you have a plan, you have to adhere to the plan no matter what may be happening and no matter how you may be feeling. Just think about how better your life would be if you changed your relationship with your possessions. That will make it easier for you to stay committed.

Whenever you buy something again, you will have a better sense of why you are buying a certain item. Now it is time to declutter and to let go of the things weighing you down.

Just Do It!

At this point, you have a commitment and a plan. You know what you have to do and why. Use to 8020 principle as there is a good chance that 20% of the stuff is responsible for 80% of your personal results. If you look at all your stuff, there is a good chance of that being the case.

Most of the stuff doesn't really do much more than being nice to look at. The 20% that contributes to your results the most is what you also use most often. These things are also likely to fullfill you and make you content o a great extent.

When it comes to the remaining 80%, you have to get rid of it and this will be easier if you list those things based on how emotionally attached to them you are. The stuff which you care the least about is the stuff you want to get rid of first. It gets trickier as you move up the list. You have to stick to the plan and think about how those things are weighing you down. This whole process is easier if you remain focused on the 20% of stuff as a source of positivity.

Don't Forget What is Important

This whole process is not easy and improvements wont be noticed immediately upon its completion. Thats just not how it is. The whole process is for nothing unless you stick to the plan since that is the only way to prevent the clutter from returning to your life after the declutter.

It is not just about getting rid of things, it is about changing the mindset and your philosophy about things and life. This is the hard and uncomfortable part. Deviate from the plan may be very tempting when you come across some new fancy gadget. This is when commitment is tested.

Decluttering isnt just about getting rid of stuff, it is also about remaining clear of previous habits and acquisition patterns.

Don't Skip Anything

It's simple to remove things that are undoubtedly status symbols. It's simple to do away with things that are clearly gadgets, trinkets, and things which really don't include very much value besides maybe some kind of mental reward. Take a look at things which give you pleasure. There's a ton to deal with there.

You need to recognize that if an object gives you pleasure, you are simply utilizing that thing as some kind of mental mirror. Genuine pleasure, confidence and a feeling of worth or significance can only come from within. You're utilizing that thing as a prop.

Your task is to get rid of the object and go directly to the root cause. It is you providing yourself that meaning. Remove the middle man. Pay attention to what's within. Shortly after you have done away with the 80% of tangible clutter, you need to begin considering all your other possessions. This could be non-material. I'm referring to mindsets, mental patterns, psychological clutter, beliefs, assumptions, fallacies.

Believe it or not, these are tougher to deal with. As I pointed out, a great deal of the physical things which we purchase are effectively just mirrors. Their true worth is based upon what's happening in our heads. They help remind us of the ideas which we hold in our heads.

Remove those ideas, and you would not require things that embodies that. As unpleasant as cleaning up a bunch of these physical belongings can be, this doesn't match up to the type of heavy lifting that you will need to do within your head.

Chapter 5: Getting Rid of Mental Clutter

As I pointed out in the intro to this book, your physical clutter sets off the emotional clutter. Emotional clutter, consequently, sets off other manner of inner clutter, which drives you to participate in hoarding habits, or whatever else can result in physical clutter.

This tangible clutter then speaks to your inner clutter, and the entire procedure replays itself again. You're transmitting all the negative signals to yourself, and you wind up considering and carrying out things which steer you additionally down this hole.

You need to take the following step and take care of this inner clutter. Or else, despite the amount of stuff you eliminated of your life, you are going to ultimately return to where you began. By and large, the tangible clutter which we create or stockpile in our lives is just a stand-in for our emotional concerns.

We purchase things not due to the fact we require it but due to the fact we read all kinds of meanings into it. In case you are searching for a car, you could do equally as well purchasing a Kia. It keeps you nice and cozy, and dry whenever it's raining outdoors. Simply put, it deals with the basics, however folks don't purchase Kia's. Rather, they crave and want Lamborghini's, Ferrari's, BMWs, Mercedes Benzes, Maserati's.

In short, you're not actually purchasing stuff due to the necessities that purchase tackles. Rather, you're purchasing stuff thanks to the emotional signs or mental reality you're reading into. There is a call-and-response pattern here. You purchase things due to the fact that you're feeling unfulfilled within.

The more things you possess, the more you require since you keep nourishing that emotional gap that is constantly craving. You need to take care of that emotional gap after you've dealt with the physical part of clutter. You do this by changing your mentally upsetting habits. This is the initial step.

If you invest a great deal of time with social media, that is not a good use of your energy. When folks publish their updates, they're displaying to you images of their "perfect life." No one will upload video footage of them getting fired from their job or any other event that is just as bad. No person does that, at least no one in their right frame of mind.

Rather, what you get are pictures of the parts of their life which are heading the right way. You get a wonderful photo of a family heading out for dinner. Everyone outfitted really nice. You get delightful, underhanded pictures of the new BMW in the garage.
They are going to think of imaginative ways to let you learn about their new achievement. Perhaps someone would post "Have a look at the new bicycle I got," and they have a truly lovely, decent-looking bike, and directly behind it is a Bentley. You know how this works.

Sadly, if you saturate yourself in that sort of stimuli, you are captured in a social signal "soup". You're basically comparing the actuality of your life with the misleading truth proposed by other folks. It's a losing game. They're in excellent shape considering that they're presenting you the aspect of their life that is proceeding in the right direction. They don't display to you HIV or cancer or addictions. They demonstrate to you the ideal part of their lives. As a matter of fact, a bunch of folks who do this, do it to comfort themselves. They're just saying to themselves, "Somehow some way at the very least one thing is going well in my existence."

The issue is you're absorbing this all up and the message that you're receiving is: "My life stinks compared to that person." The comical feature of comparison, at least in a social media framework, is that irrespective of what you possess and no matter how good you have it going, it is never going to ever amount to what you are seeing. Whenever you compare and contrast, you find yourself on the losing side since you don't concentrate on whatever it is you have. Rather, your focus heads to what's lacking, and it all leads to the identical destination. You don't have enough.

That's the story you keep instilling in your brain when you participate in emotionally straining habits such as social media. Even if you were to get rid of your Twitter or Facebook accounts, you're nevertheless going to encounter this if you associate with folks who boast about stuff that's working out in their lives.

A ton of individuals who do this don't actually do this to put you down. Actually, a great deal of them feel truly unconfident and without control. Therefore, what do they do? They accentuate the aspects that are going their way. And here you are absorbing it all in, and you take anything they say literally and because of that you wind up missing out. You find yourself coming up short. That's the way comparisons function.

This is a quite harmful environment, and you don't need to be on social media to experience this. You ought to tone down or get rid of your social media accounts, and you ought to stop spending time around toxic individuals.

The Bottom Line

Removing emotional clutter truly comes down to monitoring what you feed your emotions. You need to recognize that whatever you pick up has an impact on your mental state. Sadly, a ton of folks are really negligent concerning what they feed their brain. They believe they're merely checking out what's going on and catching up.

The issue is if you possess the inappropriate perspective, you wind up placing yourself in a more stressful spot. It doesn't truly matter what you have going your way. Assuming that you possess the inappropriate attitude, you are going to always find yourself at the losing end of that contrast.

Even the most productive and wealthiest people on the planet can make themselves feel depressed by means of comparison. Stay clear of that comparison frame of mind. It's fine to socialize with a bunch of folks, but if your attitude leads you to do this, at that point you deteriorate yourself. Monitor what you feed your mind with.

It all comes down to your attitude. When folks are saying anything to you, you could definitely interpret it a neutral way. You could also read it in a constructive manner. You could place a twist on it that elevates you, motivates you or invigorates you. This is easier said than done. Actually, folks interpret things in the worst manner conceivable and they feel worse when it comes to themselves.

Bear in mind who you involve yourself with, what you concentrate on and, essentially, how you interpret things. The trick to this truly all comes down to taking care of your emotional habits. A great deal of our mental habits are passed down from our parents. We are, besides, primarily products of our enviroment.

Nevertheless, simply due to the fact that your past is a particular way doesn't essentially indicate that you need to die with that same past. The big undertaking of life is to conquer previous programming. you were born in poverty and coping doesn't automatically indicate you have to die like that. It all comes down to observing what you give to your emotions.

Inevitably, you ought to arrive at the point where no matter how antagonistic people are around you, your positive psychological patterns allow you to counteract that feedback. Rather than beating yourself up, you could perhaps even make use of this feedback to drive yourself ahead. To kick off the process, you need to initially zero in on five harmful emotional habits to reduce and after that get rid of these from your life.

Harmful Emotional Habit # 1: Regularly comparing yourself to other people

You need to recognize that folks commonly compare themselves to other people. We're sort of genetically inclined to do this. But why?

Well, imagine thousands of years ago and you and a friend are strolling down a path and one of you notices a bear. You see that your friend begins warming up as if he's exercising for a race.

You ask him, "Are you insane? You will never outrun that bear. You understand how quick bears are." Your buddy would after that explain to you, "I don't have to be quicker than the bear. I just have to be quicker than you."

This classic joke emphasizes the reality that folks are comparative naturally. Whenever people stop contrasting themselves to others, it's highly probable that they won't invest sufficient energy, and their genes are going to vanish. Even so, we arrived at an age in which a lot of our fundamental requirements are handled by technology and present-day markets. Now is the moment to do away with this default propensity to continuously compare yourself to other people.

You ought to proactively interrupt this type of thought patterns. One of the absolute most effective approaches to mess up comparative thinking is to become more outward-directed. For example, if you end up seeing an old friend you haven't seen in a while, make an effort to be more enthusiastic and say, "You haven't aged one day", without making any comparison between you two.

Transform your evaluation and your psychological focus on the other individual. This is among the ideal things you could possibly do since not only does this make the other individual feel far better and this could go a very long way in sealing your relationship. It additionally refocuses your thoughts from your usual inclination to compare.

Direct more of your interest to other people. Be a lot more outward-directed. Simply put, be more caring. When you have the ability to accomplish this, you're evaluating yourself less.

Harmful Emotional Habit # 2: Drawing Mental Prizes from Material Belongings

Whenever you take a look at the things which you own, stop examining them in emotional terms.

When you take a look at your most-prized belongings, appreciate them depending on their own inherent properties.

Rather than looking into the logo of the vehicle which sits in your garage and ways in which that logo evokes all kinds of "elite" or "status" images, value your things for what they perform and the issues they deal with.

Take a look at the smooth lines, also check out the remarkable engineering and you're just admiring how incredible the makers are. You get out of your cycle of worry and your necessity to continuously reinforce self-esteem.

Rather, you get pulled into a remarkable technological trip consisting of the sort of engineering required to get into the item. Do you see how this works? The identical goes for any other type of luxury product.

Whenever you do this, you concentrate not just on the product but also the individuals responsible for it. You're making wonderful progress the moment you begin imagining along these lines due to the fact that you're no longer thinking of yourself.

Typically, when folks take a look at status symbols, they consider the item actually like a mirror. They take a look at the bag which has an item logo on it and consider how rich they are, how other individuals would admire them etc.

None of this mental dialogue actually has something to do with the bag in itself. It's just about you, and the more you concentrate on yourself, the more you're caught on that ego void, and it worsens as time goes on.

Begin considering material things on the basis of their terms, not based upon the mental rewards you receive due to the fact that you have them. This is the way you make progress in your quest to owning things rather than having things own you.

Harmful Emotional Habit # 3: Immediately Thinking that a Hefty Price Tag Indicates Higher Value

A bunch of folks mistake price with value. Prices are established by means of demand and supply. Whenever there is a constrained supply and there a considerable amount of demand, the price increases. In a similar way, even when there's a substantial supply, if the demand is substantial enough or consistent enough, the price increases.

This likewise works in reverse. A bunch of folks have this notion that demand is basically a product of need. Whenever the price of pasta or wheat, for instance, increases and folks presume that it's as a result of need. The reality is that demand could likewise entail perceived demand. Simply put, the assumption of value by folks demanding a specific product due to the fact that in economics there is something known as substitution.

You could be assuming that the demand for wheat is fixed, however, you need to also bear in mind that folks are able to substitute or switch rice, potatoes or other types of wheat for starch. I introduce this to your awareness due to the fact that a large aspect of demand consists of group perception. The more you could persuade folks that a particular item has worth, no matter how plentiful that item is, its price is going to increase.

A typical instance of this is the diamond industry. Did you know that diamonds are in fact quite plentiful? That's correct. This crystallized sort of carbon is really not that uncommon. However, because of the DeBeers cartel working out of South Africa in addition to long-running, extensive advertising campaigns, diamonds have ended up being very pricey.

It should not be as costly as it is. This is because of fabricated demand. Just because a thing has a higher price doesn't always imply it has worth as far as you are concerned. Its greater cost might be because of some kind of group deception like diamond price.

When you view Ralph Lauren print advertisements, they make an effort to get you to invest into a way of life. A great deal of these photos just present certainly attractive people in spectacular locations and perhaps some of those individuals would be sporting the actual product that's being promoted.

Rather, you see this truly captivating model looking to the side like he or she has a concern. This is deliberate. The true item here is the way of life that you're expected to invest into since it's so incredible, it's so separate from your way of life. Your life is mundane. These models' lifestyles, however, are exotic.

They are appealing to what's lacking in your way of life. Your life consists of nine-to-five regimens. You turn up to work, you work your eight hours and then you head home. Rinse and repeat. Absolutely, every now and then, you embark on a vacation and have a go at anything fresh, but that's your life.

That's how they advertise to folks. Abercrombie and Fitch turn this into a scientific discipline. They show you this different life which you might have, and you experience it the second you purchase their goods. This item is the entrance to this way of life or adventure.

You just have to take a look at the billions of dollars being invested annually or lifestyle marketing to get your truth. The worst component to this advertising is that it delivers the point that your life is not sufficiently good. There is something superior out there, but you have to purchase our item to arrive.

If we take people's word that they really purchase things since it fits well, the truth is that there are heaps of other apparel lines out there which fit properly. What makes this company any different? It truly all comes down to marketing.

Nonetheless, if you take a look at the fabric, the design and whatever else, it's truly tough to warrant shelling out $200 on a pair of jeans when you could purchase it for $30 from a different brand or a no-name brand. The difference is in the sold lifestyle.

I bring this stuff up since this is what pumps up perceived value. It's smart. It reveals the genius behind these large brands but, eventually, there's very little distinction between a $300 pair of jeans and a $30 pair. They need to fool folks into believing that higher price implies high value.

Taking into consideration that there is a multibillion-dollar high-end goods industry stretching throughout various industry verticals tells you everything you have to understand about how prevalent this programming is. The smartphone you have in your pocket is proof positive of this. If you're just trying to find features, you most likely would be better off with an android mobile phone that costs all of $50.

There's truly no convincing reason you ought to shell out more than $500 on a smartphone that has a lovely little logo. Regretfully, this results in emotionally harmful habits. You must never beat yourself up over the reality that you can not load your life with high-price-tag products as price isn't always an indication of value.

The only worth any product can deliver is the worth you give to it. This procedure again shows how the marketplace functions since pricing systems don't work based upon the amount of work someone invests in a product.

Karl Marx is completely incorrect. Based upon his book, Das Kapital, the true price of any item is the amount of work that is invested there. Even if you invested two thousand hours to developing a product, however, when you place it on the marketplace, nobody wishes to purchase it. How much money is that product actually worth? A great deal of nothing.

Pricing is established by demand. The price of something is anything that you read into it. It stems from you. You must bust the fabricated link around price and value which is established by the other individuals. You beat yourself up to purchase that item since you wish to be highly valued.

You have your own inherent value. No matter what you wear. Think about your own self like a hundred-dollar bill. If I had a hundred-dollar bill before you and spit on it, trample on it with my boot, fold it, toss it around, how much do you believe that hundred-dollar bill is worth?

It's still a hundred dollars. Certain folks are going to grab it since they recognize value when they experience it. The identical goes for you. You might be dressed in rags. You might seem all disorganized. Nevertheless, you still possess value. Always keep this in your mind. Now, the key to all of this is the only individual that uncovers your value is yourself. If you act like a high-value individual, folks are going to value you. In the end, this really all comes down to your choice and your judgments.

Harmful Emotional Habit # 4: Focusing on "Drawing Out" the Benefits People Have Rather Than Viewing Them as Whole People

Do you socialize with folks who are energy vampires? These individuals socialize with you only to absorb your positive vibrations. They don't add a thing. All they speak about are their issues. They spend time around you because they wish to feel great. You speak of things that are heading in the right direction, and they cruise on this positivity. These individuals are drawing out good energy from you.

They view you merely as a host. They are energy barnacles. You perhaps do this too at a certain degree or another or in one style. It's really uncommon that you encounter someone who only likes to socialize with you due to who you are. They possess a great deal of abundance in their life, and it streams to the outside.

Sadly, the majority of folks are not like that. Rather, we socialize with people to obtain things. Now, it would blow to associate with folks who attempt to squeeze money from you. Nevertheless, this takes one other shape. These are individuals who are psychological vampires. All they talk about are their issues. They discuss matters that are not going well.

In addition, other individuals like to stir your own insecurities due to the fact that they're unconfident.

They hope that by talking about their frustrations you will talk about theirs. These folks only wish to believe that there are other individuals as unhappy as them all over the world.

Perhaps at first, it feels awesome. But, the more you activate each other's pessimism, the further you create harmful psychological energy between you. Rather than your friendship allowing both of you to leave this emotional hole, you really wind up giving one another shovels.

You need to dispose of this particularly harmful emotional habit. Why? The more you draw out from someone else, the less probably you will fix your own troubles. All you're accomplishing is just assuring yourself with what is primarily bad in your life without truly doing this to fix it at long last.

You're certainly not challenging yourself. Rather, you're enclosed deeper inside your comfort zone, and you're just reiterating this pessimism or you're drawing out some kind of emotional peace of mind from your buddy.

Hazardous Emotional Habit # 5: Freeloading Emotionally Off People

Have you ever socialized with folks who think just like you? You might be considering that this is a beneficial thing. Sadly, that sense of belonging has limitations. There is something as a comfy prison. Whenever you're hanging out with folks who just strengthen your worst assumptions, you're not really helping yourself.

You wind up speaking and preaching to the choir. No one advances. No person challenges their viewpoints. No one enhances their possibilities of bursting out of this psychological imprisonment. You need to recognize that psychological prisons end up being more limiting when folks who reside in the network with one another.

There is some kind of emotional reward. Nonetheless, you're paying a strong price for it. You're strengthening one another's preferences. If you do not trust me, focus on a friend who you are emotionally freeloading off or who's doing so to you. Keep track of the topics you speak of. I'm ready to wager a great deal of money that you discuss the identical things over and over again.

This is harmful. You're not challenging one another to leave the emotional mess. Rather, you're again allowing one another dig a much deeper hole. Partly, this is actually comparable to the five harmful emotional habits I explained above. A great deal of the folks who have those damaging emotional patterns are the identical as individuals who I'm going to illustrate.

The results are identical. They lead you to an unpleasant place. They strengthen all your nastiest emotional habits. Identify the following five kinds of harmful people in your life and begin distancing yourself from these guys. This does not always indicate that you need to cut them off completely. You just need to grant yourself ample distance.

You still chat with them every now and then, but they're not so near and so dear that they wind up pulling you down. At the minimum, you're not so attached to them that you are caught in this descending emotional spiral.

Harmful Personality Type # 1: The Black Hole

This individual has deep emotional requirements. They're really needy individuals. You can't tell by their look. Some appear quite successful. Nevertheless, when they open up their mouths to someone they believe that they can count on, it's all about them, them and them.

It's as though any sort of support, any type of convenience or any type of emotional help simply won't measure up. Even though you provide and provide, it's nonetheless insufficient since that's how they are. They are black holes. Do yourself a big one. Steer clear from black holes. I'm not claiming that you ought to cut them out, but don't get so close. Why? Picture a spacecraft or a planet getting next to a black hole. What do you think happens?

Harmful Personality Type # 2: The Judge

Do you have a buddy or an associate who's regularly placing everyone and everything into neat, orderly, small boxes. This may not appear all that damaging initially. Nevertheless, this habit of theirs could be quite harmful since existence is not black and white.

It's easy to believe that when someone develops a negative opinion that it's unreasonable contrasted to when someone has a fantastic impression of you and states, "Oh, you're a champion." Well, suppose I informed you that they are equally harmful? Why? People are people. We change constantly. There are numerous edges to us and to minimize somebody into a one-word summary really empties them of their humanity.

Regrettably, none of the subtlety matters to the judge. He or she obtains a significant amount of pleasure in rendering his or her world as black and white as feasible. Either someone is a loser or someone is a winner. There's no midpoint. You don't essentially need to stop being pals with these people, but attain some kind of space because, eventually, you begin embracing that black-and-white frame of mind, and this is very destructive due to the fact that the world is not black and white. It's actually so vivid, so dynamic and so stunning.

Harmful Personality Type # 3: The Stylish Hoarder

The style hoarder is an individual who checks out various people's lives and looks for patterns or styles which they can gather. When you talk with this person, they're not truly curious about the genuine you. They couldn't care less concerning your expectations, goals, fears, ambitions, insecurities.

Rather, they evaluate what you are doing. They're consumed with all kinds of trends. These could be technical trends, style trends. Nonetheless, it's things which various other people are doing.

They then utilize this as some kind of framework when they're judging you, and they claim, "Ah, this person, does he think in this manner? Does he cooperate in that trend? Does he have this style understanding that is sort of trendy?"

You pretty much prove their verdicts regarding trends since they're drawing out a large awareness of their self-worth and pride from that. They really feel great about having the ability to identify these trends. They feel good about belonging to the appropriate group or individuals who think the appropriate ideas.

However, the inspiration is very superficial. It's truly all about making themselves feel great, feel significant and feel deserving. Sadly, this is all at the exterior level. They do not truly have the primary principle or the substance of the trends which they are so engrossed with.

Whenever you socialize with these folks, you end up being shallow too. You begin slicing and dicing individuals based upon where they are in regards to politics, societal sensibility, principles, etc.

However, people are more than the sum of their parts. You can take someone and segment that individual to various levels, but guess what? Whenever you piece all those strata jointly, they don't amount to that individual. Something's lacking.

Perhaps we can call this the spirit. Irrespective, the reality is you can't simply dismantle people based upon these patterns and reconstruct them into a comprehensive person. You overlooked the individual.

That's just how these individuals think. They view it as level after level of things that they are able to recombine, reconfigure, and slice and dice, combine and fit. If you spend time these individuals sufficiently long, you end up being like them. Regrettably, that type of believing flops when it comes to the truth since folks, essentially, are not like that. We're worthwhile even more than the aggregate of our parts.

Toxic Personality Type # 4: The Troll

Internet trolls are frustrating. Nevertheless, the issue is they're not continuously apparent. As a matter of fact, one of the most popular sorts of trolling entails flattery. There are folks who believe 180 degrees reverse of whichever view or personal opinion you posted. They couldn't differ with you more, however, you can not tell according to their answer.

It appears like they're encouraging you. Nonetheless, what they're truly doing is trolling you since they don't agree with what you think. They're doing this for giggles. They get a twisted feeling of fulfillment in being total and complete liars. Nevertheless, the issue is that trolls at some point reprogram themselves.

It's not rare for a troll to get such a jolt getting folks to agree with matters that they themselves despise since this makes them dislike the individual or mock the person in their thoughts. Ultimately, they get so caught in their choice that they no longer recognize what the reality is. The entire extent of the game is just to get a surge or a response from people.

Rather, it's just the emotive thrill that they're receiving. "The individual is agreeing with me, and he's a total and complete moron and a dogmatist. I gotcha!" Who do you think pays the greater cost? The individual who is at least truthful with his/her viewpoint as undesirable or unpalatable as it might be, or the individual who lead him on?

Keep in mind that if you participate in this behavior, you're really selling your soul. I'm referring to your integrity. The nastiest component to all of this is that the lie ultimately permeates in and ends up being you. It enters into you. You get to a place where you don't even know which side is up. That's how puzzled trolls are.

It all comes down to nourishing insecurities since they're quite unconfident at some level or another. That's why these guys take pleasure in getting folks to claim things that they despise or say things that they deep down within wish to say.

Due to their habits, support and deceptive tactics, they get individuals to articulate out things that they wish they might say or stuff which they detest. Associating with these individuals draws out the worst in you. Furthermore, you wind up with someone who doesn't truly value you for who you are. If you're not cautious, you may wind up being like these folks. Their whole life is a lie.

Eliminating emotional clutter necessitates in your emotional habits in addition to a confirmative choice to keep away from people who have a tendency to strengthen those unfavorable mental habits. A great deal of this stuff can be fairly understandable, but it's certainly not effortless to do.

The bright side here is that you don't need to attain complete freedom from these emotional patterns and these individuals overnight. You simply have to choose to take baby steps and stick to those actions. Permit yourself to be persistent. The bright side is if you keep applying constant initiative, ultimately, you are going to become free.

Once again, please keep in mind that this doesn't imply that you need to cut out a great deal of folks from your life. You just have to place some distance between you and them so these guys do not emotionally deteriorate and taint you.

Chapter 6: Getting Rid of Emotional Clutter

Watch what you feed your mind. You need to be watching your habits and taking note of the folks you socialize with. While this is necessary, you also need to ensure that you take in the right sort of stimuli.

In any given day, we subject our own selves to all kinds of data. Surprisingly enough for the large bulk of these inputs, we are totally oblivious. There are regularly details that we notice, smell, taste, tap and listen to. Nonetheless, in spite of the countless daily stimuli we go through, we really just get to memorize a small portion of them.

Of these recollections, we only evaluate or judge an even tinier fragment. Among these recognitions, only a tiny percentage will make it to our personal story. Mostly, they either strengthen things which we currently think we understand about ourselves, or we just recall them, contemplate them, concentrate on them and ultimately lose sight of them.

Now you might be considering that this is totally ordinary. Mostly, you're correct. But the issue is that we can easily subject ourselves to all kind of stimulations which produce psychological clutter.

Now, these are separate from emotional clutter. Emotional clutter sets off your sentiments about your spot in the world, what you're about, what you can do, your connection to people, so on etc.

Psychological clutter, however, entails psychological regimens that form your personal story. How you read things generates emotional conditions. Deciding on how you opt to evaluate these stimulations takes a fair bit of effort. You need to be conscious of how your mind works.

This is where eliminating psychological clutter truly serves to help. When you police the stuff which you feed your mind with, you can recognize your psychological procedures and nullify them if they were in opposition to you.

What to be conscious of? Like I pointed out previously, we soak up all kinds of thing during the day and you need to really categorize these items utilizing broad headings in order to alert yourself about their content.

For instance, we can feed our minds superficial forms of entertainment. This could be useless YouTube videos. This could take the format of incivilities and trolling on comment sections in addition to Twitter feeds.

These are not 100% lacking value, however, they are basically useless because they're so superficial. They don't truly captivate you on any profound level. They do not challenge your presumptions about yourself, actuality and the world. Rather, they just create some kind of emotional reward. You're enjoying yourself and that's basically it.

Another form of harmful psychological input which you ought to be conscious of involves suggestions which make you less content. It's one thing to test yourself and your occurring assumptions, it's another to take in concepts which really destroy your capacity to be content. Ideas entailing your sense of value, the value of other individuals and life as a whole.

The intriguing point about this is that initially, it begins as another kind of entertainment. You could frequent certain message boards and folks only keep repeating the words "kill yourself" or saying that life doesn't actually matter or there's truly no point to anything.

There are numerous versions of this. Now I won't question the philosophical finer aspects of such ideas. Maybe on a philosophic, logical and rational grounds, there might be fire where there is smoke. Rather, I'm just planning to concentrate on their impact on you.

It's one thing to question your beliefs so you could experience your life in a more successful way. At one level or another, we certainly have to demolish any false idols which we possess entailing a mistaken belief. That's part of maturing. But there are suggestions which could make you less content since they wear down your capability to be content. I hope you see the issue here.

I'm not referring to encountering an idea which makes you examine the religion that you're born into. That's one thing. Actually, in most cases, that's healthy. I'm not promoting atheism here. Rather, I'm recommending that people really believe what they profess to believe.

In that case, whichever religion you're born with ceases being a label which is handed down from generation to generation and alternatively ends up being truly your own. You really live out the truths taught by that system of faith. You experience it play out in your life. You see that it's the truth and it's strengthened in your mind and you purposely choose it. I'm not discussing that.

I'm talking rather about concepts that damage your ability to be content. This entails the nature of humankind and the point of life. There are some ideas around that essentially result in the conclusion that it's all pointless, meaningless and hopeless.

How could you be content if you buy into that? How can you construct anything when that is the type of ideas you envelop yourself with or when you subject yourself to online material that retells that identical destructive message repeatedly?

One more kind of input which you want to be really cautious with involves harmful emotions. If you keep encountering content which just nearly always immediately places you in a negative emotional state, there's an issue. If you're sensing a remarkable amount of negativity, you are deteriorating your individual effectiveness.

A great deal of individuals attempt to deceive themselves into believing that this is just an aspect of them being real. The actuality in their minds nearly always is negative. If it isn't negative, it's a fantasy. It's some kind of self-delusion.

Well, thinking about life in black or white turns out like this. It certainly positions you for harmful emotions. You wind up rearranging your world in such a manner that your emotional pinnacles become all the more extreme.

Ultimately, you need to keep away from time wasters. Certainly, they're captivating, fun and a bunch of people discuss them, but inevitably, they just use up an excessive amount of time. This is the time you could've devoted to improving yourself. This could've been the time that you devoted to uncovering a number of truths about yourself. Opportunity costs don't just relate to economic concerns. They likewise concern your psychology.

For each second you buy in endeavors which rob you of your time, you're losing out on something more rewarding. Perhaps you could've been performing something which might allow you to end up being a more in tune, truthful, genuine individual living in integrity.

To recover from these negative psychological ideas, you have to be forthright. Don't hesitate to designate things as they are. It might appear severe, it might even appear absurd since it ends up being perfectly obvious that you're engaged in detrimental thought patterns or enabling yourself to become introduced to this content. You need to conquer your pride and simply call things how they are and simply label them.

The more you label, the more you decide to end up being mindful, the less likely you are going to keep soaking up this data and these inputs without a dispute. At least you end up being more understanding and conscious that this is happening. Ultimately, you are going to have the ability to act on them. You are going to manage to keep away from them.

Look for and Destroy Anti Affirmations

Suppose I told you that each and every day, you are performing a script in your mind? You're not very aware of this script, but if you truly focus on yourself, you're stating particular aspects of yourself, who you are, what you can do and so on. This is what psychologists call self-talk.

Now you might be assuming that this is only a basic psychological reporting system. Like you're looking out the window and you're experiencing things play out, then you're merely explaining to yourself what you're witnessing.

There's some of that, however, a bunch of it actually is some kind of reoccurring commentary regarding who you are and what you can do. You're likewise mentioning to yourself what your capabilities are.

You need to be really aware of your self-talk since if you create a damaging habit of saying bad things regarding yourself, they emerge as self-fulfilling prophecies. If you continue repeating these bad statements whenever you recall an error you performed before, what you're accomplishing is you're reprogramming yourself to become what you dread. If you keep stating that you're a moron, then guess what? You are going to become a moron.

This all results in a self-fulfilling prophecy since you are programming yourself according to the things which you keep claiming to yourself. You need to comprehend that your mind is not only kicking back and soaking up all of this passively.

It's in fact saving it and reading it as some kind of programming and don't be shocked if your damaging self-talk winds up keeping you back and pulling you down. These are anti affirmations. You very likely already understand what affirmations are. These are phrases which are meant to give you toughness and concentration.

Sadly, we also struggle with anti affirmations and in contrast to positive affirmations, we immediately take part in anti-affirmations unless we decide to be knowledgeable about them and interrupt the procedure. We're already accomplishing this.

There are 5 standard groups of negative self-talk "scripts" you have to counteract. The initial type includes self-talk which destroys your self-esteem.

When you take part in this self-talk, you program yourself to feel less deserving. You continue judging yourself in the worst manner.

The second type of negative self-talk scripts consists of protection. When you state these things to yourself, you make yourself less and less self-assured, and less and less safe. You state to yourself, "You're constantly messing up. You don't actually know what you're doing. You're inept."

This is separate from "You're stupid" since when you say you're stupid, you are coming to the root of who you are. Rather, when you take part in negative self-talk which makes you unconfident, you refer to your abilities to perform particular things.

One more negative self-talk theme consists of your personal performance. You keep mentioning to yourself, "Well, that didn't work. Why should it work the following time you attempt?" You keep resaying this kind of script and soon enough, you're not even planning to make an effort.

You end up being a less successful individual because any type of skill, even though it's something that you understand like the back of your palm, will eventually deteriorate if you don't take part in it regularly and consistently. This generates a damaging descending spiral.

You get poor results, you feel even worse about it so you're less probable to make an effort to try again. There's a tight link created between lousy effectiveness, low self-esteem and lousy outcomes.

One more motif that you ought pay very close attention to consists of your absence of clarity. You could take part in self-talk which wears down your capability to appropriately see things for what they are.

Rather, you simply see things like a huge fog and it's all just involved in a perplexing label of your situation. One usual damaging self-talk script which individuals utilize is, "I'm just not fortunate."

I hope you can notice how this results in disarray because when you claim "I'm just not fortunate" you shut down all internal dialogue. There's no requirement for your logical and rational part to break down the facts of what's taking place in your life in such a manner that you are able to understand things.

If you simply dismiss all of it as simply a bad fortune, there's no additional analysis required. How could you analyze fortune? This produces confusion. This makes you intellectually idle since, believe it or not, things don't occur mostly randomly. Generally, the outcomes you receive are the impacts of your past decisions.

Regrettably, when you participate in self-talk like fortune, the system, or it's all a conspiracy, you produce confusion for yourself since you establish this rational haze that has certain aspects of rationality.

You wind up fooling yourself into believing that "That's all the research I require. I don't have to go any farther in assessing these core problems with my life. I simply need to go with the reality that I'm simply not fortunate."

Whenever you generate this confusion for yourself, you're truly robbing yourself of all the strength that you actually possess. Last time I checked, it doesn't actually make a difference what you appear like, where you originated from, where you are, the missteps you made previously, you could always decide to switch things around.

You could permit yourself to be operated by your visions and your optimism for the years to come so you could go passionately to create the sort of tomorrow you wish for yourself.

Ultimately, there's one more set of self-talk themes which make you psychologically lazy. This is, mostly, pertaining to the confusion that I pointed out prior, but it needs its own category since individuals have a tendency to soak these in.

Whenever you socialize with people, don't be shocked if you begin believing like them. This occurs since you soak up other people's perspectives and their manner of viewing the world.

You wouldn't do this if this failed to work on some level or other. Individuals are not dumb. You will just take in mental patterns only if they fulfill some kind of purpose. At some level or another, it operates, but the issue is you might be opting for an idea which is not all that profound.

It's not all that extensive and worse yet, you place yourself to live a life built upon assumptions. Rather than challenging your thinking faculties, you end up being trapped. You just search for particular signs and you begin jumping to conclusions.

Rather than permitting yourself to be sufficiently open-minded to really take a look at the facts and attempt to come up with various analyses, interpretations or even better, developing your own theory, you begin the game using this template in your hands and you're simply enforcing this template on whatever you encounter.

Not shockingly, the majority of the time, you come up with a poor match. Things which play out in your life fail to nicely match this intellectual template which you utilize. However, folks who carry this out can't be bothered.

They end up being mentally idle. If they encounter a pattern which has 5 things and 2 fit their assumptions, that will do. Be careful of the affirmations which match any of these 5 themes. If the things which you say daily result in these conclusions, then you're in trouble. Interrupt them.

Try to conquer them. One of the highly reliable ways is to just nullify them. What this indicates is that you state a different affirmation to substitute them rather than automatically kicking off into "Well I'm just not fortunate. I'm stupid." You turn things around and state another thing.

How to Create Affirmations That Actually Work as They Should

A bunch of other books make an effort to fill their pages with affirmations people can use, but allow me to tell you, they flop. Why? They do not know you.

The writers of those books clearly can't read minds. That's the reason why it does not make sense for them to come up with these canned lists of affirmations which work on individuals based upon particular circumstances. Rather, I will simply take you through a procedure of you creating your own affirmations which have a greater possibility of working. Why? They essentially match your set of conditions. They really emulate your track record and experience.

First, you want to exceed the standard and the superficial. When you offer an affirmation to yourself, you need to cut to the core of the problem. Rather of just simply stating, "I look excellent" think of the reason why being told you look excellent matters. When someone says that you look excellent, it indicates that they value you, see your worth and they feel that you matter.

Next off, you need to custom-tailor your affirmations based upon ways in which you really think. This necessitates that you hear yourself initially. When you state particular things to yourself, how do you express it? Do you simply say "I'm messing up" or "I scored big this time around" Focus on your actual inner dialogue and after that phrase the affirmation to suit that dialogue pattern.

Once again, this is one thing which only you are going to be able to discover. A bunch of affirmations out there openly fail since they appear so shallow, unnatural and basic. It is crucial to pay attention to how you really think. In what way do you phrase these subconscious words? In which way do you string them with each other? Now that you possess a fundamental idea of the affirmation you really wish to give to yourself, form and reshape these to match the method you usually use to speak to yourself. That's the way you get it to register.

Chapter 7: How to Get Rid of Clutter in Your Career

Another kind of clutter which you truly want to handle consists of what you do for a living. If you're similar to the common American, odds are you're not very delighted with your career.

The majority of folks that I've talked to in researching this book really despise what they work on for a living. If offered an opportunity, they would do something else. They could also take a pay decrease. That's how powerful their distress is with the things that they do for a living. This is a truly large source of clutter.

If you go to a job which seems like a daily degradation, what impact do you suppose that would have on the remainder of your life? A bunch of family abuse in fact develops from this. For instance, a father is miserable with his job, don't be shocked when he's not a really forgiving individual regarding his wife or kids.

The identical goes for the mom, and the youngsters. They're not thrilled with the school, which will likely produce turmoil across the board. So just how do you remove career clutter? Below are just some recommendations.

Decide to Love What You Do

The primary thing you may do is to head to work with the clear goal of loving what you do. Beginning at a particular date, I want you to purposely find the satisfaction, significance and value in what you do. Welcome it. Permit yourself to feel great about the things that you do.

Discovering the passion in what you're presently doing for a living is really simpler than you think. How am I so positive? Well, let's put it like this. In case your job is such a total and overall time waste, you most likely would have identified a reason to give up your job sooner.

If it truly burns you or if it truly is such a void in your life, you would've located the resolve and the strength to leave your job sooner. However, you're still there. I uncovered this when I worked for an insurance business and I had this buddy who walked in and he would just moan and groan about his job all the time, each day. As he was shuffling the documents, seeing the customers, looking through the handbooks and procedure books. Well, sure enough, the business underwent a reorganization and there were a number of months where supervisors, along with the management team, were actively assessing everybody in regards to firing or early retirement.

What do you presume my friends' response was? If he truly disliked this job, he would've been thrilled about the chance that he might get omitted since it includes a lovely, fat, lump sum in addition to retirement benefits. Besides, he's been working at that place for at least 20 years. However, he was terrified.

Throughout those months, it occurred to him that as frustrated as he was with regards to particular facets of his job, by enlarge, he loved his job. It was one of those substantial individual conclusions, but naturally, when he discussed this with me, he wasn't really emotionally sincere about it.

Because hey, let's admit it, if you've been griping about your job for numerous months or perhaps years to your friends and after that suddenly, you return with a total 180 degree different perspective of your work, you 'd seem as a fool.

But reading between the lines, I understood what occurred. It occurred to him that his job wasn't as horrible as he believed it was. Soon enough, I began seeing him smile at the office more frequently. He didn't get retrenched, but the chance of being let go eventually woke him up to just what caused him to turn up to work for well past 20 years.

If you are in a career which you think is dead-end, drains your spirit or typically feels toxic, I wish for you to halt and consider what tasks you engage in at work which keep you returning. At the very least one task gives you sufficient passion to desire to come to work day in day out, week after week, month after month.

It might have something to do with freedom. It might have something to do with the topic you're involved with. Discover the passion in what you're undertaking. If this would not get the job done for you, the next approach which I know works features gamification. This is just a lavish word for attempting to turn particular aspects of your work into a game.

Perhaps you could look into various processes which you perform and attempt to link some kind of success at the completion of a process. Perhaps you work at an office where you can effortlessly compare your effectiveness with other individuals. In that condition, you could establish a leader board. There are really no rewards here, but by considering your job as some kind of video game, you could see yourself begin at a level and advance.

You could end up going from landmark to landmark, success to victory. It no more appears like some obscure mishmash of meaningless activities which don't truly lead you anywhere. Rather, you see a wonderful straight progression and if you handle your job as a computer game with a substantial emphasis on unlocking a growing number of achievements and acquiring more points, you could be shocked to find that your boss would like to promote you more frequently.

You may be nicely surprised by how much more cash you are going to be earning. You need to comprehend that the amount of cash you're generating at work is actually the price tag your boss or the powers which be placed on the worth of your work.

Naturally, this is marked down by their profit margin, expenses, and other variables. Still, it's an evaluation of the amount of value you bring. If you employ gamification techniques to your work tasks so you end up being more productive, your work caliber increases and you can manage harder tasks, the worth of your work improves.

For quite a long time, your boss is going to be appreciating a bargain since the overall value of your production is so much larger than the amount of cash they're compensating you.

But considering that the labor market is still a market, your boss would certainly be an ignoramus to maintain this discrepancy going for too long. Ultimately, they would begin ratcheting up your payment to get a tad closer to the genuine full value of your services.

Now don't get far too excited. It is going to by no means get there, but at the very least you are going to be earning more than you are earning now. You're not simply one more face in the crowd. You're someone who really appreciates their work. You're effectively element of that core group of workers who take things to a higher level.

One more method to utilize to love what you do is to obtain a side project. You could begin an online business, perhaps it's an online store, perhaps you may check out dropshipping. Perhaps you could even freelance on the side. No matter what the case might be, you begin doing stuff on the side which makes an income.

This has the result of guiding your attention to tasks which have nothing to do with your primary job. A great deal of the tension and negative feelings which you have regarding your job can come from the reality that you simply have all this unused time. After you come home from work, you begin considering what took place at the office and you feel horrible.

Now, rather than doing so, you begin considering your side project and doing freelance work, doing creative work or online marketing, you don't offer yourself the chance to keep mulling over things that you're distressed about.

This maintains things fresh with your primary job. Ultimately, you begin evaluating it with a different point of view. It's no longer as repressive as you formerly believed.

Discovering the Courage to Let Go

Now, as strong and helpful as loving what you do can be, for certain folks, it's truly not a possibility. They just can not discover the passion in what they're performing, gamification doesn't get the job done and try as they might, their side project doesn't keep them engrossed sufficiently.

In this scenario, you need to find the tenacity to let go of your job. It's the cause of harmful thoughts which you can't get rid of, no matter how hard you try.

You most likely prefer to look at this as your first option, but I recommend you attempt to love what you do initially. If that isn't getting the job done, you need to develop a game plan to let go.

Don't participate in the game the way the majority of other unhappy employees do. They get to a point in which the straw broke the camel's back and they put in their 2 weeks notice. Rather, set your resignation at a convenient point down the road.

Ease into it. For instance, you could state to yourself, "Okay, I'm miserable with this job. It's not actually leading me somewhere. It's creating a great deal of problems. I'm planning to quit. But I give myself 2 years or 1 year." Regardless of what the case might be, you need to give yourself a good cushion.

One useful effect of this is that you understand that at some time, your income will go down due to the fact that you will quit your job. This drives you to plan better so in this manner, whatever cash you save, you are able to invest. You could handle your resources better.

You're not placing yourself in a circumstance where the date suddenly shows up and you just need to quit and your income goes down like a rock. Then get so hopeless that you get another job which is comparable enough to the previous job which you end up being unhappy again. Your job tragedy replays itself again and again.

You need to set that date, but here's the trick. Once you establish that date, stay with it. Sadly, a lot of folks try to establish phony ultimatums to themselves. My buddy, that I detailed earlier did this constantly.

He'd frequently say to me in frustration, "In 6 months, I'm going to quit." Then he would provide me with a date and state: "Mark my words. When that date arrives, I'm out of there." Certainly, that day came and went and he's still there. He was still whining and life moved forward.

You need to establish a date when you are going to take that jump. When you do this, you force yourself to plan in advance. You begin putting away cash, building a reserve and most prominently, you begin setting yourself up for a smooth landing. Possibly you could launch an online business. Perhaps you could get a job search going which results in far better work.

No matter what the case might be, you utilize that target date to drive you to action. It's not simply like some kind of psychological or emotional bookmark. Establish a date and stay with it.

Unlocking the Power of Passive Online Income

No matter if you stick with your job or you are intending to shift to self-employment, you may wish to think about putting together a passive income online business. This includes developing an online asset that you work very hard to develop. But the bright side is you work one time, but the revenue keeps coming.

Now, don't become too excited. This does not imply that there's completely no additional work. Such systems do not exist. Regardless of all the buzz which you have heard, there's no such thing as a full "set it and forget it" money system. There's still going to be some kind of work required, but it won't occupy as much time as a full-time job.

The big distinction between a passive income and an active job entails needing to work to make money. With active income, no work indicates no income. With passive income, you may work to develop the asset, relax and still earn an income.

That's where you want to be since when you quit working on one asset, you may develop an additional asset and yet another one and before you realize it, the small trickles of online income amount to a nice stream of revenue that can not just surpass your 9-5 income, but provide you a remarkable degree of freedom.

You build them up once to get them performing and you will not need to babysit them. You do not need to do work to make money unless, naturally, you get involved in freelancing, that is actually similar to working a job but on your own conditions and schedule.

The main dynamic of freelancing is still comparable to active income. You still need to do the work for you to make money. You cease working, you don't make money. With passive income, you put in enough time once and after that, the system generates revenue by itself. If you have the ability to properly establish online passive income streams, you could lead a digital nomad lifestyle.

There are numerous bloggers around who bounce from one country to the next. They tackle many various hobbies. Their blogs generate income via advertisements. Their Instagram accounts generate income via sponsorships. You could be among those digital nomads. You should disenchant yourself of the idea that there's this set massive method to earn money on the internet. I'm sorry, but unless you are considering building a startup, that simply won't transpire and typically when you create a startup, you essentially trade your life for the business.

Startups call for a bunch of time and there's truly no proof that the startup would do well even though they can consume a lot of time, work and mental energy.

Rather, I'm referring to developing small, passive money streams and these incomes are reasonably humble. You don't actually bring in all that much, but the bright side is that when you develop a lot of them, these streams amount to a fair bit of money.

This is particularly true if you enter into e-commerce by creating your own dropshipping store. If you wish to completely own your time and delight in a remarkable amount of financial and personal freedom, explore earning from internet-based assets.

Chapter 8: How to Enjoy More with Less

There's a traditional Zen Buddhist saying "less is more" Now, for the longest time, a great deal of folks were mocking this claim. This really is regrettable since there's a bunch of truth to this. How come? Well, when I was in university, I didn't have many things. I did not have ample cash left over for a lot of food, much less, belongings. But guess what? The things which I did own, I genuinely appreciated.

I recall purchasing this nightstand from a goodwill shop. I hung on to that nightstand for near to a decade after finishing university. I really ended up being connected to it not only due to its features but likewise due to the fact that it reminded me that I don't actually require all that many things when I moved from flat to flat.

That nightstand was a concrete reminder to me that it was truly my mindset that helped to make me feel content. It's my attitude which made me believe that things were valuable and complete. I discussed this with you since it's simple to think that for you to feel safe, you need to encircle yourself with a great deal of stuff. It's easy to fall under the trap of believing that for you to feel great, the things you possess have to have the appropriate logos, labels, or have to be created by the right producers.

The truth is that these things just have meaning due to the fact that you decide for them to have meaning. The meaning stems from you. As I stated, I had a nightstand which was all shambled up and didn't truly appear all that great, but in my head, it was quite valuable. You need to embrace the same attitude with the things which you possess. Because if you read that much meaning into the items which you purchase, you wind up purchasing less.

Your mind could only hold on to so several points of reference as far as meaning is concerned. You are going to manage to take pleasure in your belongings because eventually, they remind you of what's actually genuinely valuable in your life. You no longer participate in this ineffective race of just obtaining an increasing number of stuff due to the fact that you're searching for more and more meaning.

Rather, when you decide to end up being mindful of how each single existing possession you currently have provides you meaning, you feel more content. There's less of a void in your life which you want to fulfill with people, things, ideas or endeavors.

Strip Down the Things You Enjoy

The following step you ought to take entails doing a total evaluation of all the things in your life. This consists of people, events and actual things. Carefully consider the various people in your life. What do you appreciate about them? In which way do they engage your understanding of purpose and meaning? Do the identical with the endeavors you engage in. Apply the identical evaluation to the items you own.

The more you perform this, certain trends start to surface. You begin connecting the dots and it appears that individuals, endeavors and things in your life all share particular common concepts. When you can do this, you begin looking at these factors in your life for what they are. You value them. They're no more proxies for that ultimate experience which you're searching for.

They're no longer things that you need to obtain so you may feel great about yourself. Rather, you peel all down to emotional states which are real. You begin seeing these concepts interact. Appropriately, you're less probable to keep obtaining things since, at this moment, it does not make any sense.

Uncovering the Core of Enjoyment

You may possess a ton of stuff, but do you truly enjoy it? You might have a great deal of time, but do you truly enjoy the time? These questions head to one source: enjoyment. You need to ask yourself, what could you value about your life daily? What are the things which you truly eagerly anticipate? If you're entirely truthful with yourself, you should manage to find at the very least one things. Sadly, a bunch of individuals can't even get that far. A great deal of them are so baffled that they can't even identify one. Reflect on what you eagerly anticipate every day. What can you value every day?

Another method to respond to this question is to pay attention to loss. As the traditional saying goes, you just miss the water once the well is dry. Every day, you visit the well to obtain water. Actually, it's so standard and you've accomplished it plenty of times and now you don't even consider it. Obtaining water from the well is automatic.

Now could you picture a terrible drought and that water runs out? Before it runs out, you begin becoming conscious of how crucial it is. Before you realize it, the water is gone. You remember its value. Consider particular difficult times in your life where you lost things, people, or you were not able to participate in activities which you typically do. What can this inform you about what's significant to you? What should be essential to you? What does this reveal you about the things which you ought to be appreciating?

Fixate on the process of enjoyment. When you're appreciating something or the company of individuals or indulging in an activity, attempt to break it down into a declaration which you are able to articulate. No matter what the case might be, note down reasons why you enjoy particular items, particular activities and precisely why being around particular folks feels so nice.

After you've jotted down your responses, ask yourself, "In what way can this satisfaction improve the remainder of my life?" Simply put, if you manage to enjoy yourself in some situations, why not take things all the way? Why not discover that degree of satisfaction in other parts of your life?

Whatever You Do ... Do This

I know what I will say is simpler said than done. I know that you come with all kinds of obligations, responsibilities and duties which really necessitate your focus and you're unable to completely enjoy life and reside in the moment. I recognize that, but no matter what happens and how you do stuff, at least make an effort to do this.

Attempt to create good memories. At the moment you may be worried. You may be fighting with deadlines or other minor fires or crises occurring in your life. Even so, enjoy what you're working on since when you take a snapshot of what's taking place in your life, ultimately some of it would make it to your memory banks.

I recognize it seems like a cliché, but life is really a lot shorter than you want to admit. I know, at the moment, you're most likely trying to maintain your head above water in particular parts of your life, however, attempt to take psychological snapshots of where you are.

Make an effort to fixate on those aspects of enjoyment. Believe it or not, you are going to arrive at a point in your life from where you look lovingly back to them. Ultimately, at a particular moment in your life, you are going to understand the power of memories.

Unlocking the Power of Memories

Typically, when folks consider memories, they usually view it in practical terms. You recall stuff since it allows you to perform particular things in the future. You recall how to perform things, you remember particular days. It's designed to result in some kind of practical advantage.

Nonetheless, it's also effective in regards to your feeling of meaning and happiness. When you discover how to uncover the power of memories, you are going to have the ability to remember things willfully. It resembles watching a film from the past and as you most likely already know, whenever you see a whole lot more details in a film, you are going to manage to combine it together to a greater degree.

This has a really strong practical impact on your life. Part of the reason why a lot of us are so burnt out, afraid and miserable is the reality that we truly have defective memories. We fall short to see things in context. Remarkably, we blow things out of proportion, we concern ourselves regarding matters which have yet to occur, even though we've observed that pattern play out a lot of times prior.

The issue is memory. If you can willfully recall patterns and particulars from the past, you would certainly feel more responsible. Things won't appear as turbulent or as enormous or as insolvable as they seem at the moment. When you can willfully recall things from the past, your recollections could provide you the motivation you require to calibrate your filter.

The main reason why we have a tendency to react detrimentally now is since we have embraced poor filters at some time in the past. Whatever the case might be, we possess a poor filter. Sadly, we only uncover that it's poor when it's far too late. A greater approach would be to truly emphasize our capability to recall so our filters are clear. We immediately discover that our filters are not helping us in any way.

We organically realize that our filters are working in opposition to us rather than for us. For this to take place, you need to have the power of remembrance. You need to have unmistakable memories.

Lastly, if you were to place a bunch of focus and time on recalling your past better, this could result in mindful filtering. I trust this much is clear. All the procedures that I've explained lead to the conclusion that we are engaged writers of our reality. You need to recognize that the inputs the world is transmitting you are neutral. It is you who assigns them meaning.

We may do this passively or consciously and proactively. Nonetheless, it will take place. Sadly, a great deal of the aggravations folks have about their lives is because of the reality that they're just not aware of their individual filtering process. They only allow it to hit them. They believe that this is the reality since this is how their brain typically works. It doesn't have to result in that conclusion.

You could knowingly filter the inputs that are coming in. You could alter what you concentrate on and of these stimuli, you could alter how you decipher them. Lastly, you can transform what you decide to recall and how this connects to your personal story. That's how strong your mind is.

Unfortunately, you won't gain from this if you struggle to be aware of it and you fall short to take command of it. When you keep training your power of memory creation and recollection, ultimately, you begin filtering your reality in a really mindful way.

Chapter 9: Learn to Be Content

I wish I can say to you that there is some science to contentment. While there is a fair bit of science entailing issues focusing on contentment, in the end, it's an art. It's sort of like baking a cake. Anyone could break down the ingredients. Folks could do a great job explaining the pattern in which you mix, fold or otherwise deal with the ingredients.

But as you most likely already understand, there's a great deal more to it than that. What accounts for the distinction? Art. Art truly is all about dealing with your specific set of conditions and these conditions change as time go on. You yourself also evolve over time.

Life is an art. And naturally, one of the greatest tasks which we need to plunge into includes contentment. To end up being content, you need to care for it like an art. There's no special formula.

Rather, it's an art. And much like with every other art form, there are particular attributes which you ought to seek. Use these features. Make them get in touch with your specific individual reality and your specific circumstance for things to work out. With sufficient initiative and consistency, matters are going to fall into place.

Enough is Possible

The primary thing which you are going to find out when you look at contentment as an individual type of art is that there is something akin to enough. At the moment, you're believing the opposite. At the moment, you're experiencing all kinds of aggravations confronted with so many obstacles precisely due to the fact that you don't think that you possess enough or that you suffice.

You need to enable yourself to believe that there is a mindset of enough. In the absence of this belief, you will simply be taking chances in the obscurity. You will simply keep on struggling needlessly for an unbelievably long pace of time.

Permit yourself to strongly believe that there exists such a thing as enough. The moment you enable yourself to swear by the concept of enough, things begin to take shape. You're no more managing this confusing haze of emotions, disappointments, worries, depression, tension. Rather, you begin sealing things. You begin placing restrictions to things. You're no more shadowboxing with ambiguous ideas.

After you believe that enough exists, you at that point also need to believe that it's completely fine to stop desiring after you have attained that state of enough. This is the way in which you arrive at contentment. Sadly, there is no mystical formula which precisely takes you from point A to B.

Achieving Emotional Contentment

When you permit yourself to believe that there exists such a thing as enough, then the following step is trusting that you are able to be happy enough. Being emotionally content does not need to comply with some kind of gold standard which stays the same during your life. Rather, being really emotionally content truly hinges on your circumstances.

The circumstance will alter your interpretation of contentment, but at the very least if you're open-minded to it, you are going to have the ability to attain that especially if you need to wait for assistance to reach where you are.

The sole thing which is able to change is the way in which you choose to view your scenario and this is where emotional contentment appears. Ideally, everyone would be earning a million bucks a year, but that's not real life. We need to mentally make peace with what we possess.

At a certain level or another, we need to desire the reality that we possess. This is where emotional contentment can be found. It's a confirmative decision on your part. And it develops from the unyielding faith that there exists such a thing as enough. Typically, you think in terms of more, more, more.

Psychological Contentment

Whenever you permit yourself to feel that you have more than enough and that you are deserving enough, you are able to attain psychological contentment. It truly all comes down to your self-esteem. If you believe you're good enough and things are good enough, you need to permit yourself to halt.

This doesn't imply you need to stay there forever, but you need to rest. It's fine. Rather than draining all this mental energy attempting to assert some kind of control, you recognize that it's fine and you begin transmitting energy in a more concentrated and straightforward way.

In a way, attaining mental contentment is not a whole lot different from someone who is treading water. If you know how to swim, you realize that when you tread water, you could kick and move your legs around in a really minimal manner to remain afloat. You utilize less energy while maximizing your floating time.

Psychological contentment is a nice place to be at. You don't need to drain mental energy by returning to stuff, stressing over stuff, yanking stuff from your memory banks, distressing over them. Rather, you will have the ability to focus on the present moment and enable yourself to remain in the moment.

Spiritual Contentment.

If you discover the art of contentment, you begin evaluating your spiritual facet in a more favorable light. I don't wish to sound rough, but a bunch of modern folks frequently deal with spiritual concerns in physical means.

When you attain some degree of spiritual contentment, you make peace with the reality that there are some things in your life which you simply can not describe. You agree to them with what initially seems like an uneasy truce. Ultimately, it begins to sink in.

You begin noticing the outlines of the aspects of your life which form your spiritual hole. You could, at that point, take care of them in a more relaxed and less nerve-racking way. Everyone has a spiritual edge since essentially, this part of our self talks to our necessity for purpose and meaning.

Letting Go of Attachments

By this point, you ought to have conducted a fair bit of de-cluttering. Once that occurs, you would, at that point, be in a place to grant meaning to that absence of clutter.

This all brings about the problem of attachment. The main reason why we have a tendency to accumulate a bunch of stuff is due to the fact that we assign all kinds of meaning into them.

Ultimately, we get so adjusted to this meaning that we effectively establish an attachment to the things which theoretically create that meaning. Actually, those things are just mirrors. The meaning really originates from us.

At this point, you will zero in on this truth and take the conscious, deliberate and positive step of letting go your power of attachment.

The moment you accomplish this, you punctured deceptive assumptions concerning the source of your safety, assurance and personal pride. Now I wish I can inform you that this is really easy and simple. It seriously is not.

The difficulty is not integral or belonging to the act itself. What makes it hard is your personal attachment. The bright side is you can conquer that by straightforward dedication and decision. Keep deciding on letting go of attachment.

Initially, you may trip up, however, if you carry on, sort of like water dropping on solid rock, eventually, you are going to make a hole in that rock. Ultimately, the solid rock is going to succumb to the water. You need to do the identical with attachment in your life.

Overcome These Enemies of Personal Change

I'm suitably aware that you're truly managing significant issues. As a matter of fact, you've grown familiar with them across the course of numerous years. The bright side is if you enable yourself to end up being accustomed to ways in which you, yourself, would resist, you could attain excellent progress.

Whenever folks attempt to make the adjustments which I explained in this book, their thoughts actually run in predictable means.

By deciding to get prepared for them and coming with a prepared response, you could go a very long way in pacifying them and getting away from their impact. But if you allow them to strike you like a ton of bricks, you might be so shocked and so unready that you return to your old behaviors.

I will just outline 3 situations here, but they ought to give you enough insight in how your brain is going to attempt to handle the adjustment which you're attempting to impose on your life.

First, don't be shocked if your brain informs you that being content indicates you're being a loser. The belief being that genuinely vibrant lives of superiority call for constant struggle, conflict, and work. Anything short of this indicates that you have missed out and you are a loser.

This is false. As a matter of fact, being really content is the sign of a winner since not only are you saving energy, however, you're concentrating energy to where it really has to move. The best way to end up being a loser is to burn yourself out by continuously chasing after your tail.

One more thing you can state to yourself is that being content indicates you are going to be abandoned. This is a deception which accentuates your need for external validation. You determine your success according to the lives of other individuals. But that's exactly the type of believing that got you into this hole from the beginning.

You're so concentrated on other individuals' expectations on you that you have forgotten what really matters to you. As a matter of fact, things might have become so bad that you are effectively living someone else's life and desires.

Being content does not imply you're getting abandoned. As a matter of fact, being content indicates you're establishing your own life's rate and you're assuming control of it for once.

Eventually, be ready for the concept that being content suggests you are decreasing your standards. This actually is only a variant of the concept that a life worth living needs to include continuous struggle.

While it holds true that to really get your life to a higher level, you need to battle against particular problems in your life. You need to confront particular challenges. But this is different from believing that you need to do this day in and day out. If you were to undertake that, at that point, your life is just one large conflict. It's simply this black hole of tension.

Contentment is the accurate reverse of reducing your standards. Since you have discovered your standards and you have determined what is deserving and meaningful, you allow yourself to become content.

Conclusion

This book has set out how to discover to de-clutter your life on various levels. This book has likewise shown you the value of contentment. As amazing as these suggestions are, they won't do you any good if you only keep contemplating them. For them to transform your existing individual reality, you need to act on them.

Questioning how you think is a step. It's not a mental-emotional workout since it has a direct impact on how you function as well as on whatever it is you say. You need to become involved. You need to choose a date, get ready for that date and no matter what happens, begin on that date.

This likewise implies that you need to organize things right. This book has offered you a framework, however, it truly is only a sketch since you need to complete the details. Not just am I not a mind reader, I simply cannot enter your life and produce the difficult decisions which have to be made for true and successful transformation to take place. The only individual who can do that is you.

This calls for preparation and focus on details. Most importantly, this needs devotion. How crucial is devotion? Well, you really need to maintain it since real transformation doesn't transpire on a "one-time big-time" basis. It's not like you perform a bunch of activities for one week and all of a sudden, your life is significantly different.

This is not a movie. This is your life and usually, you have to make little modifications which scale up with time. This is a compounding effect in which you invest in particular activities and choices each and every day and their cumulative effect increases with time.

Having said that, for you to profit from these impacts, you need to continue performing them for a prolonged time period. Compounding, it goes without saying, is not simply a phenomenon you notice with your checking account or stocks. Rather, it also plays out in your routines. It plays out in your everyday tasks and choices. A tad of consistency goes far.

You might be feeling that you're not actually investing that much energy or you're not doing a lot of remarkable things on a daily basis. That's fine. Provided you're putting in the work, just as long as there is consistency in your activities, the outcomes is going to scale up over time.

I hope that you enjoyed reading through this book and that you have found it useful. If you want to share your thoughts on this book, you can do so by leaving a review on the [Amazon page](). Have a great rest of the day.

Printed in Great Britain
by Amazon